A GUIDE

TO THE PRINCIPAL

CHAMBERED BARROWS

AND OTHER

Pre-historic Monuments

IN THE ISLANDS OF THE MORBIHAN, THE COMMUNES
OF LOCMARIAKER, CARNAC, PLOUHARNEL,
AND ERDEVEN; AND THE PENINSULAS OF QUIBERON
AND RHUIS, BRITTANY.

BY

W. C. LUKIS, M.A., F.S.A.,

Fellow of the Royal Society of Northern Antiquaries, Copenhagen; Corresponding
Member of the Société Polymathique du Morbihan; the Société Archéologique
de Nantes; the Société de Climatologie Algérienne; &c., &c.

RIPON:
PRINTED FOR THE AUTHOR, BY JOHNSON AND CO., MARKET-PLACE.
1875.

In the interest of creating a more extensive selection of rare historical book reprints, we have chosen to reproduce this title even though it may possibly have occasional imperfections such as missing and blurred pages, missing text, poor pictures, markings, dark backgrounds and other reproduction issues beyond our control. Because this work is culturally important, we have made it available as a part of our commitment to protecting, preserving and promoting the world's literature. Thank you for your understanding.

DEDICATED, BY PERMISSION,

TO THE

RT. HON. THE EARL STANHOPE, D.C.L., F.R.S.,

PRESIDENT,

AND THE FELLOWS OF

THE SOCIETY OF ANTIQUARIES,

LONDON.

CONTENTS.

ROUTE A. To the Ile-aux-Moines. A chamber with a bent passage; sculpture; barrows of the Late Bronze or Early Iron period. Part of a large circle. Chambered long-barrow..................................page 4

ROUTE B. To the Islands of Gavr' Inis and El Lanic. Chambered cairns and sculptures; remains of large circles..................................page 8

ROUTE C. To Locmariaker. Many dolmens, sculptures, and cup-markings; great long-barrows with chambers; and menhirs..................................page 10

ROUTE D. To Carnac. Dolmens; chambered long-barrows; sculptures; cup-markings; lines of menhirs and circles..................................page 15

ROUTE E. To Plouharnel. Dolmens; many chambered round-barrows; sculptures; cup-markings; lines of menhirs; square of menhirs..................................page 21

ROUTE F. To Quiberon. Lines of menhirs; circle; rock shelter, with cup-markings..................................page 29

Vannes. Museum of the Société Polymathique du Morbihan..................................page 30

Peninsula of Rhuis. Menhir; dolmens; immense round-barrow with chamber; sculptures..................................page 30

Remarks..................................page 33

List of lines of Menhirs in the Morbihan..................................page 35

Index.

PREFACE.

I HAVE written the following pages chiefly as a Guide for those Tourists who desire to visit one of the richest districts of Europe in monuments of a Pre-historic age. I passed a portion of seven summers, four of them being consecutive, ending with the year 1872, in exploring the neighbourhood of Auray, and in making myself acquainted with all the principal monuments. As I was not pressed for time, and had no occupation to hinder a daily ramble over the country, which I accomplished chiefly on foot, I became familiar with most parts of it; and therefore venture to think that this little work will be no inadequate Guide for those who wish to see and to know whatever is most worthy of being seen and known.

During the lengthened period of my sojourn in the Department of the Morbihan, I had opportunities of meeting with many Tourists from England, Prussia, Austria, Spain, and America, as well as from all parts of France, and I observed that by far the larger number of them were attracted to it by its widely-famed Rude Stone Structures. There were a few among them who seemed to take more interest in Ecclesiastical, Military, and Civil Architecture than in earlier monuments; and there were others, ordinary Tourists, who had no definite object in view, or who desired to be present at some of the great religious gatherings, or Pardons, and to take a brief glance at the manners, customs, and holiday costumes of the Bretons.

For the first of these classes this Guide is principally intended. There are numerous French and English guide-books which will fully meet the requirements of the two other classes of travellers; but I know of not one in either language which enters into sufficient detail, without being too prolix, and is calculated to assist the student of pre-historic antiquities in his search after those monuments which exhibit the most instructive features. I do not for one moment imagine that this little work will take the place of any of the numerous useful general guide-books which already exist, and it is far from my intention to aim at this. My desire is simply to supplement them by pointing out the readiest mode of access to the localities where the tourist may see good examples of typical monuments,—to direct his attention to their characteristic constructional features, to inform him of the results of the exploration of some of them, and to tell him where he may find and examine their contents. And I desire to do this because those books are deficient in these particulars, besides being erroneous in others. In some of them the errors of previous writers are repeated, and the erection of these monuments is explicitly attributed to the Druids. In others one monument is confounded with another, whilst some of the most interesting and important are not mentioned at all; and some others were published before careful researches had been made, and are therefore of little value to enquirers at this time.

It was always a source of deep regret to me to observe the hasty step with which archæological tourists passed over the country, as though their great object was to see as many monuments as possible in one day, and not to study and learn. To this reprehensible precipitancy may be attributed the sadly defective knowledge which is conspicuous in many professing antiquaries both at home and abroad on the subject of chambered-barrows, and it is evident that their small experience, thus gained at full gallop, is in some measure due to the guide-books whose directions they follow. That otherwise excellent work, "Hand-book for Travellers in France," published by Murray, which is extensively used, errs in this respect, because it suggests that two days are sufficient for Carnac and Locmariaker, in which time the traveller is supposed to be able to visit, not only the important monuments of those two Communes, but also the islands where other attractive ones exist, and the very instructive structures of Plouharnel and Erdeven. It is simply a physical impossibility, to say nothing of the very cursory and therefore profitless inspection which he could make of the few monuments he may chance to see. The same work is of little value to the archæological student so far as it relates to the monuments themselves. The accounts given of the groups of stone pillars arranged in lines in the parishes of Carnac and Erdeven, are misleading by their inaccuracy, and the grave-mounds, and so-called dolmens, or as they are called by Englishmen cromlechs, at Locmariaker and elsewhere, are likewise erroneously described. With the exception of a brief allusion to Mont St. Michel, Carnac, and to two or three other monuments, the traveller receives no assistance from it.

If the Traveller desire to learn something from his visit to this wonderful district he should devote to it not less than a week, bearing in mind the French proverb:— "*Qui trop embrasse mal étreint.*" Nor should he place confidence in the directions of the hotel-keepers, who know next to nothing of the antiquities of their neighbourhood, or in the drivers of the hotel vehicles, many of whom are only employed during the summer months, and are merely acquainted with the main roads and the few monuments which happen to be along their course, and from whom very scanty information can be extracted.

From Auray the following excursions may be taken, and the monuments which may be seen in each excursion will be found treated of in this little work in the order in which the routes appear here.

ROUTE A. To Ile-aux-Moines.

ROUTE B. To the Islands of Gavr' Inis and El-Lanic, or Tisserand.

ROUTE C. To Locmariaker.

ROUTE D. To Carnac.

ROUTE E. To Plouharnel and Erdeven.

ROUTE F. To Quiberon.

The Island excursions will afford the traveller the opportunity of seeing both circles and dolmens.

The journey to Locmariaker will fill him with wonder, and impress him with awe, on beholding gigantic tumuli and enormous menhirs.

The visit to Carnac will make him acquainted with three groups of rows of menhirs with their attendant circles, as well as with tumuli of no mean proportions.

The Plouharnel excursion will exhibit examples of several distinct sepulchral chambers contained in the same tumulus; a square of menhirs, and the longest series of lines at Erdeven; and in each excursion he will find frequent instances of rude sculptures and cup-markings.

On the peninsula of Quiberon he will find a remnant of a group of stone rows, and of a circle, as well as a remarkable overhanging rock which most probably afforded shelter to the pre-historic inhabitants, within the shadow of which rock, on a projecting ledge, a little above the ground-level is a collection of cup-markings.

From Vannes he will be able to reach the peninsula of Rhuis, and visit the great chambered tumulus of Tumiac, the largest and loftiest in the Department; the lesser chambered mound of Petit Mont, in both of which there are sculptures; and other monuments in the same locality.

Since the Guide has been written I have ascertained that Mons. Hédan has given up the management of the Hotel de la Poste, at Auray, and that the new manager follows in the footsteps of his excellent predecessor.

vi PREFACE.

Explanation and Derivation of Terms.

DOLMEN, from the Breton Dol, or Taol, or Tôl, a table, and Méan, or Men, a stone. A stone table.

CROMLECH, in Breton Kroumlec'h, from the Breton Kroumm, curved, and lec'h, or léac'h, or liac'h, a sacred stone, a circle of stones.

MENHIR, from the Breton Méan, or Maen, or Men, a stone, and Hîr, long. A long or tall stone. A pillar.

Explanation of Names.

Bé-er-Groah, Tomb of the Fairy.
Klud-er-ier, Perch of a fowl.
Mané-Bras, Great hill.
Mané-er-Groah, Hill of the Fairy.
Mané-er-H'roëk, Hill of the Fairy.
Mané-Lud, Hill of ashes.
Roch Breder, The Brothers' Stone.

ERRATA.

Page 4, line 12, for late bronze read *early iron*.
Page 5, line 36, for jasper-bead read *jasper bead*.
Page 6, line 35, for Madme. read *Madame*.
Page 14, line 28, for chloromelanite read *chloromelanite*.

A GUIDE TO THE PRINCIPAL CHAMBERED BARROWS AND OTHER PRE-HISTORIC MONUMENTS IN THE ISLANDS OF THE MORBIHAN, THE COMMUNES OF LOCMARIAKER, CARNAC, PLOUHARNEL, AND ERDEVEN; AND THE PENINSULAS OF QUIBERON AND RHUIS, BRITTANY.

IN order to reach the chief points of interest and attraction in the vicinity of Auray, the tourist should make this picturesque little town his head quarters. Arriving by the railway, conveyances from the two hotels will meet him at the station, which is about one mile distant from the town. He will find comfortable accommodation at the Hotel de la Poste, or at the Hotel du Pavillon d'en Haut, the former kept by Mons. Hédan, and the latter by his widowed sister, Madame Malézieux. Mons. Hédan is an active, enterprising man, at once farmer, miller, landowner, banker, and hotel master, obliging, attentive, and thoughtful for his guests, and possessing the further recommendation of a sufficient knowledge of the English language to be able to come to the relief of an English tourist who has a limited acquaintance with French, and is shy of displaying his proficiency before others. At both of these hotels he will find vehicles for his excursions.

The monuments of the Pre-historic age, examples of which can be seen in the excursions, may be thus classified.

1. Menhirs, or pillar-stones, arranged in rows forming avenues.
2. Menhirs arranged in circles.
3. Menhirs in a square.
4. Menhirs standing singly, or associated with tumuli.
5. Tumuli containing chambers composed of rude blocks of stone; and chambers partially, or, as in rare instances, entirely denuded of their enveloping mounds, commonly called Dolmens in France, and Cromlechs in England.

6. Tumuli of the Bronze age, which are, however, of rare occurrence.

As these monuments are scattered over a wide district, it is desirable to direct the tourist's attention to certain routes, by taking one or other of which he will he enabled to examine many of them; and for this purpose he will have to take a boat occasionally.

ROUTE A. To the Ile-aux-Moines.—*Monuments to be seen on the way:*

1. At Kernoz, a chamber, with a bent passage, wholly enclosed in a tumulus. Sculpture.
2. Tumuli of the late bronze period, near the preceding.
3. Chambered tumulus of low elevation and unusual construction, on the same ground.
4. At Baden, a stone of peculiar form.
5. In Ile-aux-Moines, part of a large circle (?)
6. Near Kerno, an uncovered chamber.
7. On Penhap, a long barrow and chamber. Sculptures.

There are three ways of arriving at this island. 1.—By carriage to Locmariaker, and thence by boat. 2.—By boat from Auray. 3.—By carriage through Baden to Port-Blanc, and across the ferry. The first is not the most convenient, nor the most economical as regards time and purse. It will occupy rather more than an hour to reach Locmariaker, and the length of the sea passage will depend upon the state of the tide and the quarter from whence the wind blows; and on a calm day, upon the rowing powers and the temper of the boatmen. The length of time left for inspecting the monuments must depend upon all these contingencies; and it sometimes happens that the excursion terminates in nothing more than a tedious boating adventure, very trying to the nerves and patience of the tourist, and to his entire disappointment.

The second is very pleasant when the tourist is fond of boating, and an admirer of river scenery. The views are extremely varied and pretty; but there is the opposite side of the picture, viz., a long voyage, and a not more certain accomplishment of his object than by the previously mentioned route. The author has tried the different ways, and knows their attendant difficulties. The third is therefore recommended as being by far the best, and the easiest of accomplishment, and it will enable the tourist to see monuments which are worth seeing on the road, and to time his return to Auray with tolerable accuracy. Should there be any ladies with him, who have a nervous dread of boating excursions, they will be spared some anxious moments by taking this route. It is, however, right to add that part of the journey will be along narrow lanes, in which they will experience a fair amount of jolting.

To render him quite independent he is advised to provide himself with a well-stored sandwich box, or basket of provisions. Supposing then that he decides upon adopting the third way, he will start by eight o'clock in the morning, traverse the suspension bridge which spans the river of Bonno at Kerisper, and turning to the right, visit the chambered tumulus which is situated on a small piece of rocky moorland in front of the house of Madame Bain (du Rocher) whose husband explored it in the year 1844. The distance from Bonno to the hamlet of Kernoz, just beyond which it stands, is very short. This is one of the most interesting monuments in Brittany, and is less visited than it deserves to be. The tourist should not forget to take a few candles and matches, or he will be precluded from viewing the interior. On entering he will notice that the passage is bent at nearly a right-angle, of which peculiarity there are a few other examples in the Morbihan; but only one, that at Kergonfals, Bignan, in the north of the Department, is, or was before its exploration, in as perfect a condition as this specimen of Kernoz. That which is known as the "Pierres Plates," Locmariaker, is another, and near the village of Luffang, Crach, and on Mané-er-H'loh, Locoal-Meudon, are other examples. Mons. Bain found a few objects in this chamber, which, down to the year 1872, were preserved by his widow, but as they were then for sale, they may have passed out of her hands. They consist of a jade, and a blue jasper-bead, a flint knife, a flint arrow-point, and some fragments of coarse pottery. One of the supports on the north side of the chamber is faintly sculptured with a device resembling a cartouch. A brief account of this monument has been published by the late Mons. Louis Gallés, of Vannes.

Near to this tumulus are some mounds of low elevation, one of which was excavated in 1868 by the author and his companion, the late Mr. P. Lauerbach, of Paris, with the kind co-operation of Madame Bain's family and friends. It is a cairn, and proved to be of the Early-Iron period, and was the more interesting on account of the rarity of sepulchral mounds of this date in the Morbihan. A bronze bowl of thin metal, much corroded, was found in the centre, resting upon a reed matting, and surrounded with burnt human bones. Two iron rings, each of one inch in diameter, were in the bowl, which was filled with fine earth. A description of this excavation has appeared in the Bulletin of the Société Polymathique du Morbihan, printed by M. L. Galles, of Vannes. A second small tumulus of this group was explored in 1872 by Mons. L. Galles, aided by Messrs. F. Bain and Platel. A bronze vessel filled with human bones (burnt), and a flat bronze basin inverted over it as a cover, were found. The vessel rested on a considerable mass of charcoal, and was enclosed in a heap of stones. The same gentlemen examined two other small barrows of this group, but with no interesting result.

On the further side of the great tumulus they also explored a barrow of slight elevation, which presents different features from the preceding, and appears to belong to the Bronze age. Its diameter is fifty-five feet nine inches, and at a distance of ten feet from its base there is a circular containing-wall, composed of small nearly contiguous stones, one foot high, leaning inwards. Touching the circle at its north-east point is a structure resembling a small dolmen, which may have been a sepulchral chamber, or the entrance to a tomb which has been removed. Within it was a chipped flint. At a few feet to the south-west, two groups of bronze bracelets, twelve in each, similar in form to a large number found some years ago in Madme. Bain's walled garden, were met with; and a little further a bronze bracelet of a spiral form, and a finger-ring of copper. These objects are deposited in the Vannes museum. It has been thought desirable to introduce here the account of these discoveries, because, as stated above, of the extreme rarity of tumuli of this period in Brittany, and of the strong presumption that this diminutive dolmen, or fragment of one, is the only example in the country of a building of this class which belongs to that date. Mons. Galles has written and published an account of his finds.

Pursuing his journey, the tourist will retrace his steps to Bonno, and shortly after arrive at Baden, where there is nothing deserving his notice which need detain him, unless it be a carved block of granite, which in 1854 stood in the churchyard, and was outside, under the west wall, in 1872. It is hewn into the form of half an eliptical disc, seven inches wide and sixteen inches high, and is ornamented along the flattened circumference with three parallel roll mouldings. Whether it was intended for a Christian sepulchral memorial, or for a pagan boundary-stone, it is not easy to determine. Such stones are found in churchyards, by roadsides, and in fields. If the tourist feel any interest in this kind of monument, he will discover several in his excursions around Auray. There are a few dolmens in the vicinity of Baden which he will not have time to visit.

Arriving at Port-Blanc, he will be ferried across a narrow channel in a few minutes to Ile-aux-Moines, for one halfpenny, and landed on a point not far from a village where, on making enquiries, he will be directed to the so-called stone Circle of Kergonan. Thirty-four stones are arranged in the form of a horse-shoe or segment of a circle, the chord of which is 321 feet 10 inches in length. The monument encloses houses, fields, and a walled garden; and on its east side terminates abruptly at the road, beyond which the ground dips so rapidly that it is difficult to imagine the circle ever having been, or intended to be, completed in that direction. The average height of the stones is about six feet, and the loftiest measures ten feet six inches. A half-hour's walk from hence will bring him to Penhap, where he will see a denuded stone chamber (dolmen) at the southern extremity of what was originally a huge long-barrow (270 feet), composed principally of earth, and, its sides having been pared, now forming a high bank of separation between two fields. On the outward and inward faces of the left-hand support at the entrance of the *chamber*, he will see some rude and nearly effaced sculptures, which are supposed to represent a stone axe in its handle. There is another denuded sepulchral chamber not far from the road, between the circle and the north point of the land, near the village of Kerno. It is in a hedge, is greatly dilapidated, and is visible from the road. There are also two or three dolmens of no special interest on the island.

ROUTE B. TO THE ISLANDS OF GAVR' INIS AND EL-LANIC, OR ILE DU TISSERAND.—*Monuments to be seen on the way:*

1. Remains of a Cairn on Ile Longue, containing a long chamber. Sculptures.
2. Gavr' Inis. Great Cairn, enclosing a chamber and long passage. Many Sculptures.
3. El-Lanic. Remains of two Circles.

There are two ways. 1.—By boat from Auray. 2.—By carriage to Locmariaker, and thence by boat. The more economical of these ways is the former, but it would occupy a longer time, and as time is of consequence, the second is the preferable way.

The tourist is counselled not to linger on the way to Locmariaker by visiting the remarkable monuments that are to be seen on both sides of his road. He had better postpone his examination of them until his return from Gavr' Inis, or, better still, until another day. Should the wind and tide and boatmen be propitious, he may perhaps have time to view one or more of them on his return.

Before reaching Gavr' Inis, the island of Ile Longue will be passed, on which there is a chambered cairn, in a sadly dilapidated state, presenting some rude sculptures, which are very difficult to be seen at this time, owing to the passage being encumbered with stones. They are upon a few of the supporters and the under surfaces of some of the capstones. The chambered tumulus of Gavr' Inis is one of the most remarkable in the world. It is very complete, and most elaborately sculptured; and the proprietor of the island, Dr. de Closmadeuc, has very properly adopted measures for protecting it from wanton injury and defilement by closing the entrance with an iron door, the key of which is kept at his farm house near the landing place. The author desires to inform tourists that the proprietor, who is one of the active and intelligent antiquaries of the Department, is most anxious to afford every facility to archæologists to study this grand sepulchre. The chamber was discovered in 1832 by a former owner, but there is no record of any object having been met with when it was emptied of its contents. The visitor will be greatly struck with the elaborate and rich sculptures with which the whole of the interior, even from the entrance doorway, is adorned; and be arrested by the three enigmatical circular holes hewn in one of the left hand supports of the chamber, the use of which has hitherto puzzled all archæologists. These are cupped as if they had been intended to hold a liquid. An account of this tomb, written by M. G. de Closmadeuc, was printed at Vannes in 1864. N.B.—Candles and matches must not be forgotten when this monument is visited.

If from the summit of the cairn he look southwards, he will observe a very small island close below him, separated from Gavr' Inis by a narrow channel of sea. This small island has the appearance of a rock covered with a patch of earth. It is El-Lanic, or Ile du Tisserand, and is worth visiting for the purpose of seeing a portion of a stone circle which the restless waves have encroached upon and partly destroyed; and if the tide should happen to be low, of also seeing upon the beach the prostrate stones of a second circle of equal dimensions, and touching the first, as well as a fallen menhir still further from the shore. Dr. de Closmadeuc has commenced exploring the first circle, and already gathered many flint and other stone implements, fibrolite[*] and diorite[†] axes, knives, scrapers, hammer-stones, animal bones, and innumerable fragments of earthenware vessels. The south beach and the entire island appear to be strewn with

---

[*] Fibrolite is a mineral which is sometimes of a milk-white colour, and sometimes veined and streaked with various tints, and resembles petrified wood. It is an anhydrous silicate of aluminium, and is said to exist in thin veins in Brittany. (Damour).

[†] Diorite is the name given to a rock which is composed of Amphibole and Feldspar. When the constituent elements are visible to the naked-eye, the mineral is called Diorite; but when the same elements are invisible, and only discoverable by means of magnifying power or chemical analysis, it is called Aphanite. (Damour).

similar objects. Instead of the common pattern on Brittany pottery, which consists of horizontal streaks, or bands of diagonal indented lines made with a square-pointed tool, or, it may be, with a revolving toothed disc, the fragments which have been found here have mostly a vandyke ornament filled in with small round dots, artistically and carefully made. The rims of the vessels are also similarly adorned on their upper and inner surfaces.

It is not improbable that the encroachments of the sea, owing to a change of land-level, have separated Gavr' Inis and El-Lanic from their present respective coast-lines; and that at the period when the monuments were erected they were no islands at all, but portions of the opposite banks of the river of Vannes. The depth of water at low spring tides between these islands and the main-land suggests this, and if it were so, then the difficulty of accounting for the transportation of ponderous blocks of stone to these sites is fairly disposed of. It will be found that between Gavr' Inis and the Pointe de Bolis there is a sand-bank which at low tide is partly uncovered, and is nowhere more than ten feet under water; and that between El-Lanic and Pen-Ber the extreme depth is only nine feet. To the same gradual subsidence of the land may be attributed the destruction of a portion, and perhaps a considerable length, of the stone avenues of St. Pierre, Quiberon, where they may be traced to the edge of the bay, and where, at low tide, the stones may be detected lying in position upon the beach, until they are lost to sight under the sea. The actual channel of the river of Vannes is indicated by its great depth, which, between Gavr' Inis and El-Lanic, reaches nearly seventy feet.

ROUTE C. To LOCMARIAKER.—*Monuments to be seen on the way:*

1. Kerhan. Three Dolmens close to each other.
2. Porher. Dolmens.
3. Kercadoret-er-Gall. Dolmen.
4. Dolmen called Mein-Drein. Sculptures, and Cup-Markings.
5. Great Long Barrow of Mané-Lud. Enormous covering-stone of chamber. Sculptures.

6. Great long barrow, south from Mané-Lud, with central chamber.
7. Circular barrow with partially exposed chamber, called Dol-ar-Marchand. Sculptures.
8. Great Menhir, fallen and broken.
9. Dolmen of Bé-er-Groah. Enormous covering-stone. Sculptures.
10. Menhir, fallen.
11. Great Cairn of Mané-er-H'roëk. Chamber and Sculptures.
12. Dolmen of Pierres Plates. Chamber and bent passage. Sculptures. Cup-markings.
13. Locperec. Dolmen. Cup-markings.

There is nothing to arrest attention before passing the town of Crach, excepting a small stone on the left hand, by the road side, resembling the one at Baden, but not moulded, close to which some urns were discovered a few years ago, by M. Daniel, a farmer of the village of Kermarquer. On arriving at the road on the further side of Crach, which branches off to the right and leads to the Passage of La Trinité, the tourist may, if he likes, quit the carriage and find a dolmen or two near the hamlet of Porher. They are not of sufficient interest to be attractive; but if, instead, he enter a gate on the left hand, and walk a few steps in the direction of the farm houses of Kerhan, he will see three separate chambers so near to each other as to suggest the idea that they had all been enclosed in a common mound. It is possible, however, that there may have been three small mounds, whose bases were contiguous. A farmer informed the author, in 1866, that he had carted away the contents of two of the chambers, and spread them over his fields.

Returning to the carriage, and pursuing his way towards Locmariaker, he will observe on his right hand, in a field by the road side, at the village of Kercadoret-er-Gall, a greatly dilapidated dolmen, the mutilated capstone of which has fallen in; and a little further, near the cross of Kervarez, in a field on the left hand, a partially buried chamber, which is known by the name of Mein-Drein, where there are some faint sculptures on several of the supports, and many cup-markings on the *under surface* of the large covering-stone. After this he will come to a huge long-barrow, on his right hand, the road skirting the eastern end of it. Here he will dismiss the carriage, and meet it later in the day at Locmariaker. At the west end of this barrow, which bears the name of Mané-Lud, he will receive his first impression of the magnitude of Locmariaker stone structures. The largest cap-stone (broken in two pieces) of this still half-buried sepulchre measures twenty-eight feet in length and sixteen feet in extreme breadth. There are some sculptures on the supports; and on the large flooring slab is a device in relief, which, by some persons, is supposed to represent a bow. This great earthen tumulus, 260 feet in length, and 162 feet in width, was explored in 1864 by members of the Société Polymathique, who cut a wide trench through it in the direction of its long diameter. Near the east end they met with a slightly curved wall of contiguous upright stones, upon five of which, at intervals, was found a horse's head. In the centre of the mound a small sepulchral chamber, composed of dry masonry, and vaulted with over-lapping slabs, was discovered, and the whole was enclosed in a cairn of loose stones. This chamber contained the bones of two individuals (one burnt, the other unburnt), an axe of fibrolite, flint flakes, and fragments of coarse pottery. The chamber with its covered passage, at the west end of the barrow, has been long partially exposed to view, and nothing is known of its contents. At the entrance of the chamber is a small slab, forming a flooring stone. When it was lifted, in 1864, a small cavity was discovered, in which charcoal, a bead of transparent jasper, some pieces of coarse pottery, two flint flakes, and a clay spindle-whorl were found, and may be seen in the museum of Vannes. Mons. René Galles has written an account of this exploration, printed at Vannes in 1864. The tourist will now cross a field in a direction south from Mané-Lud, and will pass a ruined long-barrow, a great portion of which has been carted away, rendering it difficult to determine its original dimensions, but it probably exceeded 400 feet in length by 200 in breadth. Near its centre is a dilapidated chamber of no particular interest. He will then arrive at one of the most interesting and best-known structures of this locality, viz., the dolmen of Dol-ar-Marchand, which has been rendered famous by the incised representation, on a large scale, of a stone axe in its handle, on the under surface of the great covering stone, and by the peculiar sculptures in relief on the face of the large northern support. Its plan is a large chamber, to which a covered way or passage is attached. The magnificent cap-stone itself, 20 feet long by 13 feet wide, will attract his notice. This fine sepulchre is still partially buried in a circular mound. In the year 1811, human bones and charcoal, fragments of clay vessels, and a flint axe were found here.

Crossing the lane which skirts the base of the tumulus, he will see the four fragments of an enormous menhir, or pillar-stone of granite, measuring, when entire, 67 feet 6 inches in length, 13 feet 6 inches in its widest part, and 7 feet 6 inches thick. Several suggestions have been offered to account for the strange way in which the fragments lie, and for the kind of force that was exerted to place the largest and most ponderous portion at a considerable angle to the line of the others, and to roll it over. Some persons imagine that this has been effected by lightning; others that the stone fell; and others that it was rudely thrown down and broken, and its pristine grandeur purposely marred, *circa* A.D. 658, in obedience to the orders of the Council of Nantes, which required that all venerated stones, or objects of people's superstitious devotion, should be demolished. The problem is still unsolved on which end it was originally, if it ever was, erected, and whether the falling of such a mass would cause such fractures and displacements. Tourists must decide these points for themselves.

From this spot, looking in the direction of the town, a great partially buried dolmen, called Bé-er-Groah, will be perceived in a field which may be reached by crossing a few stone walls. This is a peculiar structure, and its plan suggests the idea of its having received an addition to the original tomb, the additional chamber being covered with the overlapping extremity of a gigantic stone, 27 feet long, and 14 feet 6 inches wide. It was in part explored in 1860 by Messrs. Bonstetten and L. Galles; and again in 1865 by some strangers; but besides a few Roman relics, which are in the Vannes Museum, there is no record of what was found by the second explorers. There are some nearly obliterated sculptures on two of the supports, and the under side of a covering-stone. One of them represents a celt or stone-axe in its handle, and in form closely resembles the sculptures on the cap-stone at Kercado, Carnac, and at Penhap, Ile-aux-Moines. In the same field are traces of another dolmen, and there is a fallen menhir upwards of 20 feet in length.

The tourist will now enter the town, and enquire for the key of the door which closes the entrance of the chamber enveloped in the great cairn of Mané-er-H'roëk, which is situated to the south, at a distance of about half-a-mile from Locmariaker. This mound is always described as an oval one, but it was probably intended originally to be circular. On the east side, at its base, lie two broken menhirs, side by side, one 31 feet and the other 25 feet long. This tumulus was explored in 1863 by the then Préfet of the Morbihan and M. René Galles, and a chamber of irregular form, 12 feet 8 inches by 9 feet 7 inches, was discovered near the centre, the side walls being constructed of dry masonry, and covered with two heavy stones. Near the entrance they found a sculptured slab, which is now securely fixed inside the tomb. The contents were of a most interesting nature, and consisted of 104 axes made of diorite, chloromelanite,* jadeite, and fibrolite (the largest axe measuring 18¼ inches long); an oval ring or disc (3¼ inches in diameter) of jadeite; 9 large pendants of callaïs† (green turquoise); a necklace of 41 callaïs beads; and some flint flakes. There were very few fragments of pottery, and they were quite at the bottom of the chamber, resting on

---

* Chloromélanite approaches to Jadeite in its crystalline, hard, dense, and fusible properties. It is a dark-green mineral, which, at first sight, appears black, but when the thin edge of a fracture is exposed to strong light is transparent and green. It may therefore be considered as a variety of Jadeite, in which a certain proportion of Alumina is replaced by oxide of iron. (Damour).

† This name has been given by M. Damour, a distinguished scientific French gentleman, to the mineral of which necklace-beads and pendants, occasionally found in South Brittany, are composed. In colour it approaches to emerald-green, and in its constituent elements to oriental Turquoise, from which he proposes to distinguish it by borrowing the name of Callaïs from Pliny.

the rock, and no traces whatever of human remains. An account of this monument, in the form of a Report, laid before the Société Polymathique by M. René Galles, was printed at Vannes in 1863, and the objects which were found are in the society's museum at that place.

Bending his steps for about ½ a mile in a south-west direction, the tourist will arrive at the Pierres Plates, a fine half-buried dolmen of great length, which has received this appellation from the peculiarly flat and rectangular appearance of several of the covering slabs. Here he will notice a bend in the line of the passage, and sculptures on the supporting stones of a very different character from those he has hitherto met with. It is probable that this tomb has received additions and alterations at various times. There is a stone lying on the ground outside the wall which traverses the entrance of the bent passage, on which are cup-markings. Should he have time, and desire to see other dolmens in this locality before returning to Auray, and especially should he be desirous of adding to his notes another instance of cup-markings, he will strike across the fields for Locperec, a small village at no great distance, in a north-westerly direction, where he will find, between that village and Keroulay, a small dolmen, and on the lesser capstone a series of these curious artificial indentations.

The fields around the town of Locmariaker abound with fragments of Roman tiles, and it has been supposed by some persons that this was the site of Dariorigum, or that of a considerable Roman settlement.

ROUTE D. To CARNAC.—*Monuments to be seen on the way :*
1. Near Kerhuen Brigite, the remains of a great dolmen.
2. At Moustoir-Carnac, a long barrow of large dimensions, with a chamber.
3. At Kerlescant. Thirteen lines of Menhirs, terminating with a circle. Long-Barrows.
4. At Kercado. A chambered round-Barrow. Sculptures.
5. At Kermario. Ten lines of Menhirs and a Dolmen.
6. At Menec. Eleven lines of Menhirs, with a terminating Circle.

7. Mont St. Michel. Huge long-barrow, with chamber. Cup-markings.

8. Beaumer. A surface-stone, with Cup-markings.

It is usual for tourists to undertake too much on the day when they visit Carnac, whereby they pass over much that is worth seeing. The author strongly recommends them not to extend this day's excursion to Plouharnel, but to give as much time as possible to the noteworthy objects of the extensive Commune of Carnac.

At a distance of 4 kilometres (2¼ miles) from Auray there is a dolmen, seldom visited, which lies at no great distance on the left of the road, and which goes by the name of Kerhuen Tangui. It is situated at Kerhuen Brigite, a hamlet on the north border of the Commune of Crach. The great size of the only remaining capstone (22 feet long by 11 feet wide), and the unusually large dimensions of the supports, the western being 16 feet long, render it worthy of inspection. Few of the carriage drivers know where it is, and few will aid the tourist to find it, merely because it is off the high road, and would take them out of their accustomed track. It is, however, not difficult to find. The carriage may be left on a small lande or common, and by traversing a field on foot the dolmen is descried in an orchard. At what period this great chamber was deprived of its mound, and whether it was ever explored with the spade, no record exists to inform us.

The tourist is recommended to turn to the left at Kergroix, and follow the old Carnac road, in order that he may be brought as near as possible to the stone avenues of Kerlescant. A very few years ago the carriage would have conveyed him to the avenues themselves, but so many alterations have been made in the enclosures, and so many new walls built by the present proprietor, that it is barely possible to reach them except on foot. He is also recommended to send the carriage forward to Carnac, and to make up his mind to a walk of about three miles. By adopting the following directions he will have an opportunity of seeing some curious monuments, such as are not to be found in any other part of the world, and he will be able to convince himself that what has been described and generally believed to be one monument, is in reality three separate and distinct groups of avenues.

On his way to Kerlescant he will pass near to a great long barrow at Moustoir-Carnac (278 feet in length by 117 feet in width, and 19 feet 6 inches high at its eastern end), on which a menhir is raised. In 1865 this large mound was explored by M. René Galles and his friends. A wide trench was cut through it from east to west, in doing which they found towards the west end a stone chamber (13 feet long and 6 feet 6 inches wide), covered with four stones, containing an urn in fragments; an olive-shaped object made of serpentine, incompletely perforated; a pierced roundel of blue jasper; 3 flint knives; one entire urn and fragments of three others; traces of bones reduced to a paste; and a small axe of serpentine. In the centre of the barrow was an urn, placed on the ground level; and towards the east there were two small secondary sepulchral vaults or cells, separated by a space of about 16 feet, containing nothing of special interest. These have been covered up again, the west chamber alone remains open to view.

Before the trench was filled in the section of the mound indicated the construction of this great barrow. It clearly showed that the original mound was circular, and enclosed what is now the west chamber, and that the great length to which it subsequently arrived was owing to additions which were made at various periods, viz., by the small cairn covering the urn, and then by the two cells eastward. In this manner the long-barrow of Mané-Lud, Locmariaker, was no doubt formed. The contents of the Moustoir chamber are in the Vannes Museum, and an account of their discovery by M. René Galles was printed at Vannes in 1865.

The lines of Kerlescant will be found to be thirteen in number, forming 12 avenues, and of no great extent. They reach from the village of the same name, in a westerly direction, for about 1000 feet, although it is supposed that they formerly extended far beyond the village. A few of the stones at the west end are of large size, and here will be seen the remains of an irregular circle (300 feet in its greatest diameter) terminating the series. The circle was planted with fir trees in 1869, and when they are grown, it will be very difficult to recognize it. On its north side is a long barrow (310 feet) of low elevation, partly destroyed for the sake of its materials, which have been employed in the construction of the roads and fences. A supporting wall of thin flags, leaning inwards, runs along the north and south sides. At its west end is a lofty menhir.

In a field on the north side of the lines stood, before 1868, a most remarkable and interesting chambered long-barrow, which was excavated about the year 1848, in a careless and partial manner. The barrow (150 feet long) still remains, but nearly all the stones of the chamber were sold for building purposes in 1868. It was a long narrow chamber (54 feet by 5 feet) divided into two nearly equal compartments by two upright stones. A capstone, partially displaced by the giving way of its southern support, was at the west end, and a second near it had fallen to the floor. All the others were gone. Admission into the last compartment was gained through a small oval hole (2 feet, by 1 foot 8 inches wide), cut out of two contiguous supporters on the south side, and a similar opening, somewhat larger, was made between the two stones which separated the compartments. It is said that a covered-way or passage formerly led to the south opening, and there is every probability that it was so. There is an arrangement of a like kind in a long narrow chamber between St. Pol de Leon and Roscoff, Finistère. These two compartments, when first explored, contained a large number of urns of all sizes and qualities of ware, from a dark coarse clay to a fine red, richly ornamented. At that period dolmen pottery was not esteemed valuable, and in this, as in other instances, was flung aside. The author, having obtained permission to examine the heaps of excavated earth in 1867, found very large quantities of broken vessels, and in addition a beautiful fibrolite axe, three flint arrow-heads (one triangular and two barbed) a pendant of rock crystal, a second pendant of clay-slate, and several flint scrapers and flakes. These objects are in the British Museum. A description of this barrow, with a plan and drawings of its contents, will be found in the Journal of the British Archæological Association, vol. xxiv., p. 40 (1868).

Descending the western slope of the hill on which the circle stands, and crossing the road, the tourist will enter a small fir plantation, and ascending through it, veering somewhat to his left, will soon discern the small stones of a second group of avenues, running in a westerly direction, over a rocky moorland. A single lofty menhir is planted in the midst of them. By following them he will reach a dell through which a streamlet trickles, and taking a lane to the left will find himself at Kercado. At the château, he will ask for permission to see a chambered tumulus which is close at hand, and the proprietor's servant will bring candles and admit him, for which service a small gratuity is expected. This barrow was explored in 1863 by M. René Galles, with the active co-operation of the Préfet of the Morbihan. It measures 65 feet 6 inches in diameter, and had an elevation of about 10 feet, which was reduced by the explorers, who commenced their labours by digging downwards from the summit. A fine example of a square chamber with its covered passage was discovered. The tourist is directed to notice the method here adopted for obtaining head-room by placing layers of small stones over the supports, and resting the capstones upon them. On two or three of the supports, and on the large capstone, there are some faint sculptures. On the last is a representation of a stone-axe in its handle. The explorers found burnt human remains, charcoal, two small stone-axes, three rude stone pendants, and a perforated round stone, flint flakes, a bead of serpentine, seven necklace-beads of jasper, and many fragments of pottery, all of which are in the Vannes museum. A report of the exploration, by M. René Galles, was printed at Vannes in 1863.

The tourist will return by the same lane to that point of the avenues where he diverged, and passing by a windmill, will arrive at their western termination. This group of lines is about 4000 feet in length, and is commonly known as "the avenues of Kermario." There is now no terminating circle, but it is conjectured that one formerly existed.

The lines are ten in number, and the stones at this point are of great size. A ruined dolmen, about which are traces of the mound, occupies a position in the exact direction of the extreme south line.

From this spot he will perceive the stones of the third group of lines trending westwards; and by crossing a few fields will find himself at their commencement. These he will follow, crossing the new road to Carnac, until he reaches the terminating circle at the village of Menec. This group is 3376 feet long, and consists of eleven lines. The circle, whose longest diameter is 300 feet, encloses cottages and gardens.

From hence he will bend his steps to the great tumulus of Mont St. Michel, on the truncated summit of which a small chapel has been built, and the view he will obtain will well repay him for the walk he has had. With his back to the sea, his eye will travel along the mysterious lines of pillars he has just left, and turning southwards he will see the great barrow of the Tumiac towering over the peninsula of Rhuis on the one side, the distant islands of Houat, Haedic, and Belle-Ile resting on the horizon, and on his right the peninsula of Quiberon. This long barrow was explored by M. René Galles and others in 1862. It is 371 feet in length, 192 in width at its base, and has a present elevation of 33 feet. In the centre of the mound a sepulchral cist of irregular plan, its side walls formed of dry masonry, and a large slab for a covering, was discovered. This covering stone was found to have been split by the weight of the superincumbent mass. On its under surface are six cup-markings. The following objects were contained within the tomb: 11 jade axes, 2 being perforated; 2 larger axes of another kind of stone; 26 small fibrolite axes; 9 pendants, some of callaïs; 101 necklace-beads; flint flakes; a second necklace of very minute bone beads; and incinerated human bones. Admission to the cist is now closed, owing to the giving way of the broken capstone. The above objects are in the society's museum, and a report of the discovery, by M. René Galles, was printed at Vannes in 1862. The tourist is now quite close to the town of Carnac, where he will find his carriage at the Hotel des Voyageurs. The landlady has several callaïs beads and pendants, said to have been found at Mont St. Michel, at the period of the exploration, and stone axes, which she will obligingly shew him; and he may also see, at a public-house close by, kept by one Rio, a well-formed perforated axe-hammer, in an almost perfect condition, and one or two axes. They are worth seeing.

For the information of any one interested in the subject of cup-markings, it is right to mention the existence of a surface slab, which is covered with them, on the village green of Beaumer, at a short walk from Carnac.

By this time the sun will have nearly run his course, and the tourist will be anxious to return to Auray.

ROUTE E. To PLOUHARNEL.—*Monuments to be seen on the way:*

1. On the Carnac road, near Plouharnel. A Dolmen with side chamber. Cup-markings.
2. In the village of Ker-roh. Remains of a large Dolmen.
3. Near the village of Runusto. A Dolmen. Cup-markings.
4. On the Auray road. The Grottes de Grionec, three chambers in a common mound. Sculptures.
5. On the south of the road, not far from the preceding, a Dolmen with side chambers (Kerhiaval).
6. On the north of the road, at a short distance, a Dolmen, called Klud-er-ier, with side chambers. Cup-markings.
7. At Plouharnel, the Grottes de Roch Guyon. Three chambers in a common mound.
8. Near le Vieux Moulin. The remains of lines of Menhirs.
9. Near the village of Ste. Barbe. The remains of lines of Menhirs.
10. On Mané-Remor. A Dolmen.
11. Village of Courconno. An immense Dolmen.
12. Menhirs in a square, near the preceding.
13. On Mané-er-Groah. A Dolmen with four side chambers.

14. Ten lines of Menhirs, stretching towards Erdeven. Cup-markings.

15. On Mané-Bras. Several Dolmens and an unexplored Barrow.

There are two courses open, either to make a long and fatiguing day's excursion, and to see very hurriedly and imperfectly one or two of the many interesting monuments which are at Plouharnel, Erdeven, and Quiberon, returning late at night to Auray, or to pass a day or two at the Hotel de Commerce, Plouharnel, and examine them leisurely and carefully, in the way they should be examined. The tourist is strongly recommended to adopt the latter course, in which case he should make for Plouharnel at the end of the Carnac day. The hotel is very comfortable, and the author has made it his head quarters for the summer months of several years. If it were not for the attractions of the remarkable monuments in its vicinity, Plouharnel would never be selected for a lengthened sojourn. Nothing can be more "triste" than its almost treeless and deserted external aspect. Parish church, farm-houses, cottages, all are uninteresting, and the little Flamboyant chapel of Nôtre Dame des Fleurs, on the south side of the village, scarcely invites attention. Yet this disadvantage is atoned for by the purity of the air, by the entire sense of freedom experienced, and, when the western sun brightens up the waters of the Atlantic, by the brown sails of innumerable sardine fishing-craft which are spread over miles of horizon. The visitor who is deeply interested in the archæology of the locality, is therefore unmoved by its unsightliness, and reconciles himself to the homely, friendly, plain, and unpretending hospitality of the people of the hotel, who heartily enter into his enthusiasm on the subject of Dolmens, Alignments, &c.

Supposing, then, the latter course to be adopted, the tourist, who is an early riser, may visit several dolmens before breakfast. At a few hundred yards distance, on the Carnac road, he will see a dilapidated dolmen. It is in a more ruinous condition now than it was in 1854. At that date the side chamber had its covering-stone in place, and was complete. The end support and the covering-stone are now displaced. Within this side chamber the author found in 1866, an ornamented clay vessel of tulip form, which he has been enabled to reconstruct, in great measure, and the fragments of two other urns of coarse ware and plain character, and a flint scraper. They are now in the British Museum. On the large capstone, and on one of the supports, there are cup-markings.

The tourist is recommended to proceed a short distance along the road towards Carnac, and take the first lane on the right-hand, which will conduct him to the village of Ker-roh, in the midst of which he will have a fine example of what some archæologists, in their love for classifications, would designate a demi-dolmen. The large capstone has its western end resting on two upright stones, and the other end on the ground; a supporter, from which it has slipped, lying close by. M. L. Galles explored this monument and found nothing besides fragments of dark pottery.

Within a very short walk westwards from this spot is a small bay, at the south point of which the author has discovered the remains of an ancient manufactory of pottery. The encroaching sea has swept away a great deal of it, but he has extracted portions of triangular vessels of unusual form, bricks of various sizes, square and cylindrical, a large number being like small cup-handles, which were probably used for supporting vessels in the kiln, fragments of urns, some having a black-leaded surface similar to that found in the eastern chamber of the Grottes de Grionec, and stone rubbers. These are now in the British Museum.

Returning to Plouharnel, and following the Auray road past the Gendarmerie, he will find a half-buried dolmen on the left hand, in a field near the farm buildings of the village of Runusto. On the upper surface of the capstone he will observe several cup-markings, in their arrangement resembling somewhat the constellation Ursa Major. This monument was explored in 1866 by the members of the Société Polymathique, and a Report of the work, by M. G. de Closmadeuc, has been printed in their Bulletin. They appear to have found fragments of pottery only.

Continuing his walk along the Auray road to a distance of three kilometres, less than two miles, he will come to the Grottes de Grionec, on his left hand, and close to the road side, the village of Kerhiaval being a little way on his right hand. They consist of three separate sepulchral chambers, originally enveloped in the same mound, and now partially buried in its remains. Two of them are of considerable magnitude, and nearly parallel to each other, and the third is intermediate and at right angles to them. They were explored in the spring of 1866 by members of the Société Polymathique, and a Report by M. de Closmadeuc has been printed in their Bulletin. The following articles were found in the western chamber:—a fibrolite axe, a rolled quartz-crystal, flint flakes, two clay spindle-whorls, and fragments of several plain and ornamented urns. The eastern chamber contained two fragments of human bone, flint flakes, two clay spindle-whorls, fragments of plain and ornamented urns, some fragments having a black-leaded polished surface, and being wheel-made. In the intermediate chamber, a flint knife and fragments of pottery were found. These objects are in the Vannes museum. During the author's sojourn at Plouharnel, in 1866, he examined the excavated earth of these chambers, and found an iron arrow-head, flint scrapers, a much decomposed brass coin of Faustina, and many fragments of urns, in that which lay outside the eastern. In the heap of earth at the outside of the western chamber, he found a flint arrow-head and fragments of urns. These are now in the British Museum. In the eastern chamber there are several sculptured supports.

At a distance of about two hundred yards on the south of the road, and on a small common, there is a dolmen with side-chambers partially enclosed in a circular mound, which was explored by the same gentlemen from Vannes in the same year. They found two callaïs necklace-beads, two clay spindle-whorls, a flint knife and flakes, and fragments of several plain and ornamented urns, which may be seen in the museum at Vannes. In the large side-chamber six fine clay spindle-whorls were discovered some years before; and in the excavated earth near a small chamber on the same side, the author found some jasper and steatite necklace-beads, which are in the British Museum.

ROUTE E. TO PLOUHARNEL.

On the north side of the road, at a few hundred yards distance, there is another partially-buried dolmen, with four side chambers, which is known by the name of Klud-er-ier. This was also explored by the same party, and contained a clay spindle-whorl, a flint knife, broken pottery, and flint flakes. A rudely-chipped, unpolished, quartzite axe, resembling those found in drift beds, and a small slate bead, were subsequently picked up by the author, and are in the British Museum. On a support in the north-eastern angle of the eastern chamber, on the north side, are some cup-markings.

The tourist will now return to the hotel for breakfast, after which he will visit the Grottes de Roch Guyon, a triple-chambered tumulus at about a fourth of a mile from Plouharnel, on the left of the road leading to Erdeven. This is a good example of a tumulus enclosing three distinct galleried-sepulchres, two of which are of large dimensions. It is the author's opinion that they have been erected at different times, the centre one being the oldest, that to the east, which has a side chamber, the second, and the small one to the west the third, in order of time. The gallery or passage of the last was covered with flat slabs, but the chamber itself had a beehive vault which has been destroyed. Two gold collars were found by M. Le Bail, the late landlord of the hotel, who explored them in 1849. One was claimed by the owner of the tumulus, and the other remains in the hotel, where it, as well as a collection of fine axes and other prehistoric relics, which have been picked up in the neighbourhood, may always be seen by permission of the obliging landlady and her amiable daughters. The excavation of these sepulchres was unfortunately undertaken at a period when archæological researches were not scientifically conducted; consequently no careful record was kept, and nothing noted that might illustrate the burial customs of an early age. A short letter by M. Le Bail, dated 29th October, 1849, was read before the Nantes Archæological Society, on 2nd November in that year, and probably contains all that is known concerning the exploration. It is printed in their Bulletin, and states, that in the eastern chamber were found numerous fragments of urns, and the gold ornaments. The side chamber contained human bones, ashes, charcoal, and a large quantity of broken urns. After diligent enquiry the author believes that a small flint axe was the only other article discovered.

The tourist is advised to engage the services of an intelligent lad, to act as his guide to the more distant monuments, in order that he may be spared many unnecessary steps along intersecting, intricate, and misleading lanes. A little further on the Erdeven road he will see, near a mill on the right hand, some large menhirs which appear to be the remains of destroyed lines. They are known by the name of "Les trois pierres du vieux Moulin." On the left of the road, in the direction of the hamlet of Ste. Barbe, are the remains of avenues, the head-stones of which are of prodigious size. At the present time portions of three lines only exist, the longest of which extends 1365 feet. There is a tradition, which is confirmed by an existing plan, that these lines terminated in an enclosure made with stones arranged in the form of a segment of a circle.

The tourist should now be guided to the summit of an elevation called Mané-Remor, on which is a dolmen. From this point he will have a magnificent panorama, in which he will recognize the outlines of many artificial mounds with which he will have become acquainted lately. In this dolmen, which had been previously disturbed, the author, in 1866, found a perfect hemispherical cup (1½ inches in height, 2 inches in diameter), with a small knob on one side pierced for suspension; and the fragments of three larger urns of the same form, with knobs, not pierced, and a flint knife; which are now in the British Museum.

Following his guide, he will descend the northern slope of the hill, and make his way to the village of Courconno, or Kerconno, in which he will see the nearly wholly exposed chamber of what must have been a gigantic and imposing tomb. It is sometimes used for a stable, and sometimes as a place for bruising hemp. Cayot-Délandre, in his History of the Morbihan, states that Thurief Le Durner, an idiot, whose parents belonged to the village, lived for ten years within this chamber, and died there, at the end of the last century. Other instances of individuals occupying dolmens as dwellings for a number of years are well known. A woman furnished the megalithic chamber of La Barbière, Crossac, Loire Inférieure, and, after a lengthened sojourn, died in it. The author, in 1869, found a man living in the many-chambered dolmen of the Moulin-du-Gué, Herbignac, Loire Inférieure, and learnt from him that he shifted his bed from one chamber to another, according to the direction of the wind. By filling the interstices between the stones he was able to protect himself against the inclemency of the weather.

At Courconno two capstones are in place, the largest of which is 22 feet in length; and several of the supports which formed the side walls of the gallery or passage are lying prostrate in front of the entrance. A few years ago more of these stones existed, and some of them were on end. No record exists of the clearing out of the chamber, and of the discovery of any relics.

At a few hundred yards to the east-south-east of the village, there may be seen the remains of a square of menhirs, the length of each side being about 100 feet, of which some of the stones are yet standing. It is the only monument of this form in Brittany.

On a slight elevation of the moorland which goes by the name of Mané-er-Groah, north of the square, is a galleried half-buried dolmen, with two chambers symmetrically placed on each side of the passage. There is no existing record of the exploration of this monument. A few yards further, on the same elevation, and on the verge of a pit, are the traces of another dolmen.

Continuing his walk in the same direction across the lande, he will arrive at the commencement of the great series of Erdeven lines of stone pillars, which here consist of tall, bulky granite blocks, differing in this respect from the commencement of the other systems he has seen at Carnac. At a few yards east of these menhirs he will notice a low long-barrow. There are ten lines which the tourist is recommended to follow until they bring him to their western termination at the Erdeven road. There are a few breaks in their course, owing to the removal of the stones from the enclosed and cultivated fields, but it seems probable that they were originally continuous, and extended about 7000 feet. He will observe that the lines skirt a small hill called Mané-Bras, on whose summit are two dolmens (one has side chambers), 3 unroofed chambers very near to each other, and an unexplored oval barrow. The head stones of the lines at the Erdeven road are of large size, and many of them were displaced when the road was made. On one of the large prostrate pillars, on the west side of the road, there are several cup-markings. It is thought that a terminating circle formerly existed. From this point a single line of stones takes a north-north-east direction to a distance of 617 feet, but they are mostly prostrate. At the head of the lines not more than twenty stones are now erect, and the others lie in such confusion that, without the aid of a careful ground-plan, it is next to impossible for any one to make out the lines.

The tourist will now return along the high road to Plouharnel, which he will reach in time for dinner. As he draws near to the small chapel of St. Antoine, he will perceive two dolmens on his left hand, but they are of little interest. One of them, Le Roch Breder, was explored by the author in 1866, and contained a considerable quantity of broken urns, which are in the British Museum. Should the tourist not be a good walker, he may contrive to see some of the monuments just described by the aid of a carriage, but he must be prepared for a good shaking in the narrow and rough lanes.

ROUTE F. TO QUIBERON.—*Monuments to be seen on the way.*

1. At St. Pierre, near a mill. Remains of five lines of Menhirs, and of a Circle.

2. Between Quiberon and Port-Haliguen. An overhanging rock. Cup-markings.

3. Ancient Graves.

The next morning he is recommended to take an early breakfast, and proceed by the hotel conveyance to Quiberon. He will travel along an uninteresting sandy isthmus or falaise, which was the scene of the unfortunate royalist expedition in 1795, in which the English took part, and which had so disastrous a result. After having passed Fort Penthièvre, he will direct the driver to stop in front of the menhirs of St. Pierre, which are visible from the road, on the left hand, near a windmill. These are the head stones of a series of five lines which run in a south-east direction for a distance of 635 feet, and appear to have been partially destroyed by the encroachment of the sea. The stones are almost all prostrate, but they may be traced to the very edge of the beach, and even on the rocks below when the tide is out. At a distance of about ninety yards from the head stones, in a field on the south side of the mill, are the remains of a stone circle, which, when perfect, was 200 feet in diameter. Only a dozen stones are erect, and many of the fallen ones appear to have been shifted from their original positions.

He will now push on for Quiberon, where he will enquire for some ancient graves which have been recently discovered; and if he is interested in cup-markings, he is recommended to walk in the direction of Port-Haliguen, and when about half-way, to ascend an elevation on his right hand, where he will see a huge natural over-hanging rock. Under this shelving rock he will discover, on a projecting ledge, near the ground-level, a number of these curious indentations, or cup-markings, which are common in the Morbihan, and which the author believes are in this instance known by few persons to exist; and he is of opinion that if researches were prosecuted here, traces of pre-historic occupation would be found.

If the tourist be desirous of seeing more dolmens, he may make another day's excursion from Plouharnel, through Erdeven, to Belz, Locoal-Meudon, and Etel, in each of which Communes there are several, mostly in a ruinous condition. One of those on Mané-er-H'loh, Locoal-Meudon, has a bent passage.

If he should have a further wish to see another group of lines which, however, is neither extensive nor has large stones, and consists of eight lines, extending 446 feet in length, he will have to travel on another day, a second time through Erdeven to Belz, and over the suspension bridge (Pont Lorois) which spans the river of Etel, to Plouhinec, where he will be directed to the windmill of Kerzine, close to which they are.

When he returns to Auray, the tourist must not be deluded into making an excursion by steamboat to Belle-Ile, in the hope of finding monuments which are described in guide-books. They have all long since disappeared; some of them indeed had ceased to exist before those books were printed.

VANNES, AND THE PENINSULA OF RHUIS.—*Monuments to be seen in the Peninsula:*
1. At Pencastel. A Menhir.
2. Near the village of Bernon. A long-barrow and Dolmen.
3. Tumiac. Great tumulus with chamber. Sculptures.
4. Petit-Mont. Chambered tumulus. Sculptures.
5. Near the village of Le Net. Dolmens.

The tourist has been supposed to arrive at Auray without stopping at Vannes, or to have come by way of Lorient. He will therefore make his next halt at Vannes, for the purpose of visiting the Museum of the Société Polymathique, and of undertaking, it may be, an excursion into the Peninsula of Rhuis. If he should not feel disposed to undergo the fatigue of the latter, he must by no means omit to visit the former. In la Tour du Connétable, one of the round towers of the ancient city walls, there is a very remarkable collection of antiquities. However familiar he may be with the collections of pre-historic objects in the British, Christy, Blackmore, and other European, museums, he will not fail to be struck with the peculiar and special features of this collection. In a very small compass he will find a great deal to interest and astonish him. He will see what has been gathered out of many of those wonderful monuments which he has been inspecting, all the objects being carefully and instructively arranged; and he will at once perceive that the axes and precious necklaces are of a character, material, and form, differing greatly from those he has been accustomed to see—that the axes are made principally of fibrolite and jadeite, materials not commonly met with elsewhere, and that the necklace-beads and their large pendants, which are of remarkable beauty and rarity, are composed of callaïs, or green turquoise. There is also a fine collection of urns from the same tombs.

The Peninsula of Rhuis is much less visited than it merits, probably because tourists, like the Auray carriage-drivers before spoken of, are fond of adhering to beaten tracks, or perhaps because their minds are absorbed by the overwhelming reputation of Carnac and Locmariaker. For those ordinary students of pre-historic archæology who merely desire to learn the main features of Brittany monuments, it may suffice to have become acquainted with those which have been specified in the foregoing pages, but for others who wish to go more deeply into the subject, this peninsula will furnish several instructive examples of menhirs, partially and wholly buried chambers, and sculptures.

The most agreeable and perhaps shortest way to reach the western portion of the district, where they are situated, will be for the tourist to descend the river from Vannes by boat, taking advantage, if possible, of the ebbing tide, and to effect a landing on one of the most convenient promontories, where there is a sufficient depth of water, as at St. Nicholas Point. On the way down he will be charmed with the scenery, especially when gliding past the numerous islets which lie scattered on every side in this small and picturesque archipelago. Ile-d'Arz, and some of the other islands, possess monuments, which, however, are not of sufficient interest to detain him. The great tumulus of the Tumiac will always come into view, and, like the Loadstone Mountain in the Arabian Nights' Entertainments, be the attractive power which will draw him onwards. On landing at Pointe St. Nicolas, he will notice the remains of a fosse and vallum, probably of Roman construction, which fortified the promontory, on the east side of which is a fragment of a wall which is supposed to belong to the same period. Near to Pencastel is a prostrate menhir nearly 20 feet long. A short walk will bring the tourist to the village of Kerners, east of which are the ruins of an ancient convent, and westwards to Bernon, where are the remains of a long-barrow (100 feet), directed north and south, and a large dolmen (55 feet), of which three covering-stones remain in place.

From hence he will proceed to Arzon, and make arrangements for a night's accommodation. In the course of the afternoon he will be able to visit the Butte de Tumiac, and the cairn of Petit-Mont. The former was explored in 1853 by the late M. Louis Galles and Dr. Fouquet.[*] Its diameter is about 280 feet, and altitude nearly 50 feet. These gentlemen discovered, at a distance of several yards, in a direction east from the centre, a chamber, nearly 8 feet square, covered with one roofing-stone, which is split, and a rudimentary passage, or prolongation of the chamber, nearly 8 feet long, whose side-walls are composed of dry masonry, and are covered with two blocks, also split. The entrance was found to be closed with a similar masonry. The three supports of the western part are sculptured, one of the designs being of the nature of a double necklace. They found traces of unburnt bones and of decomposed wood, 15 fibrolite, and 15 jadeite, axes, and 3 necklaces of callaïs. For the most part the axes were found broken into two or three pieces, and it has been surmised that this was intentionally done at the period of the interment, to denote the grief of the survivors. If so, the act would contravene the generally received notion that the weapons of the deceased were laid by the side of the corpse, to be ready for use in another state of existence. (N.B.—As in other instances, the tourist must be provided with candles).

The tumulus of Petit-Mont is about 30 ft. in elevation, and when explored in 1865 by the active members of the Société Polymathique (so frequently alluded to in the foregoing pages, and who, by their zeal and research, have helped to throw much light upon the subject of dolmens and their uses), was found to enclose a chamber formed of seven supports. Here are also sculptures, and on one of the supports is a representation of a right and left human foot, traced in

---

[*] Author of "Monuments Celtiques et des ruines Romaines dans le Morbihan," Vannes, 1850; also of a "Guide des Touristes et des Archéologues dans le Morbihan," Vannes, 1854.

outline as one is accustomed to see shoe-marks and hands on the lead roofs of churches in England. There are also drawings of stone-axes in their handles. A diorite axe and fragments of ornamented pottery were found.

Dolmens exist at a short distance east of the village of Tumiac, viz., near Le Net, and in a direction north-east of the latter village at Bréhuidic and Brillac. The return voyage to Vannes on the following day will be made from the point of St. Nicholas, and its duration will depend upon the advantage taken of the flowing tide.

As the foregoing has been written chiefly with the view of assisting and informing archæological tourists, and as reference is frequently made by writers on dolmens to the monuments of Brittany in support of peculiar theories which are based upon their supposed mode of construction, the author earnestly desires to direct the attention of those who may be induced to make use of this small Guide to one or two points of considerable importance.

He desires them, in the first place to inspect with very great care the dolmens which have been spoken of here, and any others of smaller dimensions, which may happen to come in their way in their excursions, so as to satisfy themselves as to their true construction, and the class to which they belong. Some writers, affirm in the most positive terms that Brittany is "un pays á Dolmens apparents par excellence," not meaning thereby that the majority are now visible megalithic structures, but that in this country where these monuments abound, many belong to a class which were *always* visible, *i.e.*, were never intended to be enclosed in mounds of which they are able to discover no traces at all. It is a matter of great importance to scientific enquirers that their own minds should be satisfied on this point, and the author therefore requests them to observe whether it is correct to say that no vestige remains of the once-enveloping mound in those cases where the monuments are at this time much exposed to view, and to make a note of those where they can detect *none whatever*.

This careful inspection is suggested to them, not because there is any real difficulty as to the question of uncovered chambers and their relation to grave-mounds, but for the sake of adding to their experience and establishing them in the true faith. Hitherto there has been too little experience, and too much error, among archæologists, upon the subject of dolmens, and the hurried glance they have bestowed upon them has not resulted in anything that has been of value to science.

In the next place, tourists are requested to inspect the monuments with reference to another theory which it is no less desirable to efface from the pages of archæology. There are not a few persons who imagine they can discover two distinct classes among exposed monuments, viz., the one just referred to, and the other which has received the appellation of demi-dolmen, for which, as a primitive structure, there is no more justification than in the former case. Several of this supposed class may be met with in these excursions, and it is of importance that tourists should be certified by personal observation of the total absence of evidence in support of the theory. It will be perceived that monuments of this imaginary class are merely dolmens in a greatly ruinous condition, round about which are still the remains of the mounds.

A third theory has been put forth rather prominently lately relating to a remarkable class of monuments of which some striking examples are found in the Communes of Carnac and Erdeven, and fragments of others in the adjacent Communes of Quiberon, Plouharnel, and Plouhinec. These groups of rows of menhirs are so unlike the other rude stone monuments of the country in their construction; so mysterious and impressive by their vast proportions; and so deficient in those indications of destination which are manifest in the case of dolmens, that men have puzzled their brains to divine what they could mean, and have invented a theory which has been suggested by the long files of standing stones resembling a great army. As long ago as the middle of the sixteenth century the line-of-battle theory was propounded by Olaüs Magnus, Archbishop of Upsala, and has been revived by a recent writer. This is not the place in which to discuss the question, but tourists are requested to inspect the several groups of lines with this fanciful view before them. They are directed to note their plans,—how that each group constitutes a distinct and apparently independent monument, each having a different number of lines,—and how that the widths of the lines are narrower at the eastern ends, and the dimensions of the stones are greater at the western. It will be also seen that the stones composing the terminating circles of Kerlescant, Menec, and St. Pierre, are thin slabs carefully selected for their purpose, and not rude mis-shapen blocks or boulders like those employed in the lines; and that where they have not been meddled with, they are designedly contiguous, as though to make a perfect enclosure impervious from the outside, and only accessible from some point where they are in contact with the head-stones of the lines. Having observed these and other features which peculiarly belong to these lines, they will not be inclined to accept the battle-field theory as in any sense supported by, and explanatory of this class of monuments. It will be noticed that they are erected according to a plan which is nearly uniform, with a direction or orientation which corresponds, in some measure, with that of dolmens, and is indicative of some use wholly different from that of a military memorial. There are at least eleven of these monuments in the Morbihan, in a more or less dilapidated condition, which are here enumerated, besides four more in other parts of Brittany.

Commune of Locmariaker.

1. Kerpenhir (greatly dilapidated).

Commune of Carnac.

2. Menec. E.N.E. and W.S.W.
3. Kermario. N.E. and S.W.
4. Kerlescant. E. and W.
5. Crucuny. S.E. and N.W.

Commune of Plouharnel.

6. Ste. Barbe. S.E. and N.W.
7. Near Le Vieux Moulin. (Very few remains).

REMARKS.

Commune of Erdeven.

8. Near the Bourg.   E. and W. generally.   S.E. and N.W. at the commencement.
9. Near Kerangré.   (Greatly dilapidated).

Commune of Quiberon.

10. St. Pierre.   E.S.E. and W.N.W.

Commune of Plouhinec.

11. Kerzine.   S.E. and N.W.

Attention should be drawn to another fact, viz., to the direction of dolmens and lines as regards the points of the compass. It will be seen that with few exceptions the entrances of dolmens are directed towards points varying between east and south ; and that the groups of lines incline in the same direction. In the above list the orientation, as far as it can be ascertained, of each is given, starting from the eastern end, or what may be supposed to be the commencement of the system.

INDEX.

A

Ancient manufactory of pottery, 23.
Animal bones in circle, 9.
Arrow-points (flint) 5, 18, 24; (iron) 24.
Avenues. S. Pierre, 10, 29; Kerlescant, 16, 17; Kermario, 19; Menec, 20; Les trois pierres du Vieux Moulin, 26; Ste Barbe, 26; Erdeven, 27; Kerangér, 36; Kerzine, 30.
Axe, drift-type, 25.
Axes, fibrolite, 9, 14, 18, 20, 24, 31, 32; jadeite, 14, 20, 31, 32; chloromélanite, 14; diorite, 9, 14, 33; flint, 13, 26; serpentine, 17.
Axes, broken at the burial, 32.

B

Baden, stone of peculiar form near church yard, 7.
Barrows, of early-iron period, 6; round and chambered, 5, 8, 11, 13, 15, 19, 24, 25, 26, 27, 29, 32; long and chambered, 7, 12, 17, 18, 20.
Bead, jasper, 5, 12, 17, 19, 24; callaïs, 14, 20, 21, 24, 31, 32; slate, 25; jade, 5; serpentine, 19; bone, 20.
Beaumer, cup-markings.
Bernon, long-barrow, 32, dolmen, 32.
Bé-er-Groah, dolmen, 13.
Belz, 29.
Bonno, 5.
Bréhuidic, dolmen, 33.
Brillac, dolmen, 33.
Bronze bowls, 6; bracelets, 6.
Butte de Tumiac, 32.

C

Callaïs beads, 14, 20, 21, 24, 31, 32.
Carnac, 15.
Chloromélanite axe, 14.
Circle, stone, Kergonan, 7; El-Lanic, 9; Kerlescant, 18; Menec, 20; S. Pierre, 29.
Classification of monuments, 3.
Compass bearings of dolmens and lines, 36.
Courconno, dolmen, inhabited, 26.
Coin of Faustina, 24.
Crach, peculiar stone near, 11.
Crucuny lines, 35.
Cup-markings, instances of, 12, 15, 20, 21, 23, 25, 28, 29.

D

Demi-dolmen theory, not supported by Brittany monuments, 34.
Diorite axes, 9, 14, 20, 33.
Disc, jadeite, 14.
Dol-ar-Marchand, dolmen, 13.
Dolmens, inhabited, 26, 27; always visible, not supported by Brittany examples, 33.
Dolmens, with bent passages, 5, 15, 29.
Dolmens, Bé-er-Groah, 13; Bernon, 32; Bréhuidic, 33; Brillac, 33; Courconno, 26; Gavr' Inis, 8; Grottes de Grionec, 24; Grottes de Roch Guyon, 25; Ile Longue, 8; Kernoz, 5; Kerno, 8; Kergonfalz, 5; Kerhan, 11; Kercadoret-er-Gall, 11; Kerhuen-Tangui, 16; Kercado, 19; Kerroh, 23; Klud-er-ier, 25; Kerhiaval, 24; Kerlescant, 18; Kermario, 20; Le Net, 33; Le Roch Breder, 28; Luffang, 5; Locperec, 15; Mané-Lud, 12; Mané-er-H'rœk, 14; Mané-Remor, 26; Mané-er-Groah, 27; Mané-er-H'loh, 29; Mané-Bras, 28; Mein-Drein, 11; Mont St. Michel, 20; Moustoir Carnac, 17; Penhap, 7; Porher, 11; Petit-Mont, 32; Tumiac, 32; near Plouharuel, on Carnac road, 22.

E

Erdeven lines, 27.
Etel, dolmens, 29.
Erroneous theories concerning dolmens, 33, and stone lines, 34.

F

Fibrolite axes, 9, 12, 14, 18, 20, 24, 31, 32.

G

Gavr' Inis, dolmen, 8.
Gold ornaments, 25.
Graves, ancient, 29.
Grottes de Grionec, dolmens, 24.
Grottes de Roch Guyon, dolmen, 25.

H

Hole of admission to chambers, 18.
Horses' heads in barrow, 12.
Human bones, burnt, 6, 19, 24, 26, unburnt, 32.

INDEX.

I

Ile-aux-Moines, 4.
Ile du Tisserand, circles, 9.
Ile Longue, dolmen, 8.
Ile d'Arz, dolmens, 31.
Iron rings in barrow, 6.

J

Jade bead, 5.
Jasper bead, 5, 12, 17, 19, 24.

K

Kerangré lines, 36.
Kernos, dolmen with bent passage, 4, 5.
Kerno, dolmen, 4, 8.
Kergonfalz, dolmen with bent passage, 5.
Kergonan, circle, 7.
Kerhan, dolmens, 11.
Kercadoret-er-Gall, dolmen, 11.
Kerhuen-Tangui, dolmen, 16.
Kerlescant lines, 16, and dolmen, 18.
Kercado, dolmen, 19.
Kermario, lines and dolmen, 19.
Ker-roh, dolmen. 23.
Kerhiaval, dolmen, 24.
Kerzine lines, 29, 36.
Kerners, 31.
Klud-er-ier, dolmen, 25.
Kerpenhir lines, 35.

L

La Barbière, dolmen inhabited, 27.
Le Net, dolmen, 33.
Lines of menhirs, list of, 35.
Locoal-Meudon, dolmens, 29.
Long-barrows, 7, 12, 17, 18, 20, 27, 28, 32.
Locperec, dolmen, 15.
Locmariaker, 10.
Luffang, dolmen with bent passage, 5.

M

Monuments, classification of, 3.
Mané-Lud, dolmen, 12.
Mané-er-H'rock, dolmen, 14.
Mané-Remor, dolmen, 26.
Mané-er-Groah, dolmen, 27.
Mané-Bras, dolmens, 28.
Mané-er-H'loh, dolmen with bent passage, 29.
Mont S. Michel, dolmen, 20.
Mein-Drein, dolmen, 11.
Moustoir-Carnac, dolmen, 17.
Menec lines, 20.
Moulin-du-Gué, dolmen, inhabited, 27.
Menhir, great, Locmariaker, 13, 14, 17, 18, 19, 26, 31.

O

Olatis Magnus, first propounder of battle-field theory, 34.

P

Pencastel, menhir, 31.
Penhap, dolmen, 7.
Petit-Mont, dolmen, 32.
Pierres Plates, dolmen, 5, 15.
Plouhinec lines, 30.
Porher, dolmen, 11.
Plouharnel, 21.
Pottery, 10, 12, 14, 17, 18, 19, 23, 24, 26, 28, 33; ancient manufactory of, 23.

Q

Quiberon Avenues, 10, 28.
Quartzite axe, drift type, 25.

R

Rhuis, peninsula of, 30.
Roch-Breder, dolmen, 28.
Roch, bearing cup-markings, 29.
Roman remains, Locmariaker, 15; St. Nicholas Point, 31.
Runusto, dolmen, 23.

S

Sculptures, 5, 8, 9, 11, 12, 13, 14, 19, 32.
Sea, encroachment of, 10, 29.
Spindle-whorls in dolmens, 12, 24, 25.
Ste. Barbe lines, 26.
St. Pierre lines, 29.
S. Antoine, dolmens near chapel of, 28.
Square of Menhirs, 27.

T

Tumiac, 32.

V

Vannes museum, 30.
Vieux Moulin lines, 26.

W

Wood in chambered barrow, 32.

Ripon: Printed for the Author, by Johnson and Co., Market-place.

CPSIA information can be obtained
at www.ICGtesting.com
Printed in the USA
LVIC060410190719
624622LV00001BC/55